§ët §ët § ęt §ż̄ ᵟᴇ† §èt

by samantha geovjian clarke

set

published by good works media llc
portland, oregon
goodworks.substack.com
first edition

ISBN: 978-1-7330703-2-4

for M

one . dēserta

not the first man
nor the last

lay in my lap your bones-brain
strip-searched too young to learn how to skin

call it a sickness, but i have always loved the barren
thieving little minds
of those precision maladaptives

Lee Harvey Oswald, not the first man
nor the last named
for a Confederate general

no blue-blood beauty in pink Chanel and his
red blood, stained with clutching

lay in my lap your blood-brain
soak this second-hand denim
and spare the Chanel

spare

time-crouch on the bathroom floor
face spurting
contact with the ceramic
ice-cold bathwater blue beryl gaze
blue bruise

big head too precious for laps
one pulsing vein furious from time travel
visiting ghosts huddled between porcelain and tile

pathetic hollow pasteboard door
pinch finger and thumb, light twist
bridal veil for a raincoat
blue for a bridal veil

ice-over failure
crouching swaddled shrivelling
beast? certainly no
monster

brain-beaten
solitary psycho-looseness
leaking from your nose

lay in my lap your batter-brain
call it a sickness

pivot

ungraceful pirouette, leakage
no healer could be fooled
on accident

swallow, swallow
hush

batter
thighs, breasts

lay in my lap. spill
battery acid
blue
blood

inoculation by exposure
to hazardous waste
from subjection to submission
transubstantiation

call it a sickness, but
i have no wish to be spared

intrusion

as if   i could ever
when seeing —   i went blind once —
when knowing —   i went blind —

as if i have eyes
                    words i believe
                    a spiritual gift
                              speaking in tongues
                    that isn't dead

as if   anyone could see
          what is knowing if unknown
          by any eye?

as if seeing weren't itself an intrusion

life fantastic

i listened to music for the first time in weeks

today. Man Man's fourth album -
lamentations so male they're almost pathetic enough
to grind into the bruise the way i like it

you dig your thumb into your own bruises.
save a little for the rest of us - you know
there's a supply chain crisis

you can't just keep waiting for the war
to justify the contusions

or the dark glasses.
      to block out the   naked   sun more than
        to block out the judgment of the rations officer

then again, what's the difference
if the grind is too weak
if the speed is too slow
if the bottle is empty
and you still ignore me

dēserta

thinning skin, creasing folds,
schoolgirl laughter desertifying
across a face aged not by time
but, like sailing stones migrating across long-dry lake beds,
by whirling winds, shoving

surely no land longs for desert
what drive shoves, refuses with every event-betrayal in its body
to let be?

what drive hunts even the fawning?
and the poor, freudian mother
carrying shoving like snow runoff
in her every crease
while new stones sail into motherhood, with new shoving, new creases, new desert
in her image

whirling disc-spin mind
refusing dismissal,
acclimated to the dizziness, a
failure of projection
forgotten project outside the self

empathy would have revealed
motion-sickness
but inward eyes cast glaring
shadows over invisibility

what being could be at such
a lack of letting

noéotectonics

disjoint - ?   or
somehow always reflection, jump of the eye across a
bent mirror

       whatever you think
       whatever you say

                      (pal)

one undoubted thing: ( )
so close underneath as to cause a lateral fault
between breath and daring

bitter stomach chokes on its acidic sorrow,
too sickened at self-pity to line its own fragile membrane
but there is no explanation for such aversion to interastral melody

it is not the song that turns song in on itself
and the stars have a right to mourn

trembling in the caverns of his ventricles:
not enough

every asteroharmonic resonance becoming part of the phonological loop
encoding an acrid taunt in his ventral stream

when i loved him first
and hard to rule out only
i could give - too much
and still not enough

that debris was, moments ago, balled up inside his stomach, imploding on
itself like a dying star

revisit
one-sided renewal, the same polar experience
reversed   explosion as release-collapse
collapse-release
familiar like the other hand

collapse, recognizing from diametric vantage Lazarus
released into the bosom of father Abraham,
can have no wish to be spared
no release from the fatherless thirst

the chasm even the good cannot cross

no wish
god grant me only a wish
only a drop to cool my tongue

wise skin, ruled by Mercury,
spelling in braille the fragile barriers
wounds to lead the blind

limestone skin
half-disintegrated before fingers
have heard it
dyshidrotic weeping as maternal instinct
to teach the eyes

he that hath skin, let him hear

god grant me just a word
to cool my tongue

one speaking
one across to know and be known

there is no comfort for the fatherless
no *with* for the mute
no weeping for the blind

no deliverance without polar reversal

                    without gravest sin

                    unbridgeable chasm

Lazarus, risen from the dead
Lazarus, delivered from collapse
Lazarus, granted a different kind of life
Lazarus, released

opposite, collapse
an opposition with no across
by its unity
for its unity

Eli, Eli

                                   lama sabachthani?

even god, fatherless,
could have no wish to be spared

ᚠ **(fé)**

bearing the stacked off-color trace
of once-branded patching
remade and remade

in one year, it will be seven years since
contact with the iron
cicatrix of cold cruel crust

seven years, and every cell will have been remade
marked in the calendar with an over-eager star
hopeful of native skin

but patching broken and re-broken
and repatched makes for
a false jubilee

       not the first man,
       nor the last

bearing the trace of
animus revertendi
it will always be seven years

evensong

do you remember
(or is that one more way i'm alone)
when you could hear the resounding hymn being sung
by my eyes turned in your direction, before
that seeing became nothing but a shadow of itself
to you, before the voice inside you that tells you lies
began to mimic my voice, before every song i sang for you
became some way to tell you that you're right
to hate yourself

can you remember?

perhaps, for you, i was always a sin -

       not foolish, not blind, but clattering
       clean-edged lies at yourself
       in your ache for the hot heart i carried
       (not for me, but for what i felt) -

and you never forgave me for never
being able to absolve yourself

but i, darling - by loving you,
i was crying *holy, holy, holy* in your name
and god heard me, and loved you too

two . looms

apokalypsis :: alétheia

an exile in a foreign land

                    -with gratitude to Humayak Asbed and his family
                    for the contribution of his vivid words-

let the one who hears
be not too irony-poisoned to refuse the mark
of that which siphons even in name
noble beast forced into a Long March
                    again, in every way that counts
at its hand

to refuse the mark
of that which is named *Babylon*
bear in gold the trace of lost marks, stolen,
demarking the bearers as followers of the god
who became beast

marks stolen, siphoned,
borders and edges all re-traced
orphans born in foreign lands
without moving an inch

to refuse the mark
of that which is named *Gestell*
for the marked will have no rest
mark in gold the unconcealing of the lamb
that was siphoned from around their necks
in your past lives

let the one who hears say, Come!
and let the one who is thirsty come

a call for endurance
bravely rest your head upon pillows
in an unknown land

for Humayak Asbed
for John, exiled to Patmos
and for all our great-grandfathers

hēpatoskōpia

now is a time that calls for
synesthetic delocalization, for endomorphisms,
for recondation
pull out of you from deeply
fermented soils every stratum of
almost-forgotten etyma
without which the glaring accessibility
of a common language
(a dream killed so slowly we still wheel
its corpse around in daily hospice routines,
not wanting to notice it died long ago)
could draw the eye of the serpent

layer, layer, layer
mantra of poetic deniability
even the archangel's battle and
the χάραγμα too epidermal
never forget
that the earth is hollow
subterranean scabies infection scraping
burrowing into, through, underneath
and all you have is pink and gold

pink and gold it is, then,
carefully practiced soft skirting easing
massive stone by massive stone
years made up of seconds
seconds made up of stones
the dead remind me:
        more weight

the shaman knows why, on that day,
women kneel and smile
because what is it but carrying
the weight of them all

████████ agape estin
and agape holds ████████████
and does not look away

we must all become scryers now
RF-Pose: Redactions Edition
interpreters of tongues
o, come all ye remote viewers
come, ye augurs and tasseomancers
he that hath a liver tablet, let him hear

just behind the I-84 / I-5 interchange

here comes a man with a leafblower

harmonic partial to the grey-edged thrum of that
metallic motorized bloodflow
through veins that arrange its moving in
the exquisite bureaucracy of concrete

interior harmony large enough he hardly notices
the dissonance-grimace of the moon
and agnostically blows the leaves in the parking lot
into a tidy pile -

a deist, at best, when it comes to who
placed the concrete
and why

post-traumatic amyloidosis

read and reread   scanning
          for already-scanned traces
          not left in the tracks of
but   signaling forward, any *placing* or *leaving* a big question mark
          which only makes the detection more tricky -
                              to note :: placed by whom?
                              unplaced :: not noteworthy?
but there's no more choice in
reading and rereading and scanning
than there is in the possible outcomes being
signaled   signaled?   what if only brushed upon

to make matters worse
it's gone burrower

what nags and rattles and shakes and pricks and drains and loads
has also begun
       to slither slick and shivering through my tunnels
       blood-eels leaving tracks of grime
       shaped like   signaling inward

directions my blood learned to follow
as cryptic leftovers

blood so convinced of extraneity
it hunts always for traces, left
by inevitability itself

finding traces internal when endless hunting
turns up no noteworthy placement
no evidence that something exists is not, after all,
evidence that it doesn't exist
     eisegesis error → neurotic dermatillomania

things that leave pits

        minefield

        excoriation disorder

        hydrofracturing

        deep vein thrombosis

        USS *Abraham Lincoln* (CVN 72)

        ichnite

        burrow

        abandoned Cilician *tonir*

        flight 93

        discarded fruit

what looms

lying on the ground in Summerville, South Carolina, while
diamond tip mountaineering on polyvinyl chloride was churning out butter
putting to shame the cheap margarine of mp3
       that hideous digital mimicking analog in blocky pixels
       designing the ocean with lego bricks

what player-piano song would Meses make
across the tines of civilization, if such wind
still lived? because of course
if she did not die with the artisans, at the last battle-cry of the last living Luddite,
then surely the great aerophone-worker has been slaughtered without ceremony by
that always-already looming
profanity: automation

how would one even go about smashing up looms
made of open-source algorithms

discordant reflection revealing its secret: blackbody
disguised as photosphere
distinctly out of alignment with the heart

on god's green earth - what
is a door
and what is a needle

what of nephilim messengers dressed in tiny lipid-molecules
presaging the Flood with their inflammatory words

what unrounded edges, certainly no skin
and why, and from where
if not Mandelbrot's shapes

hardly recognizable to Gaia as her own progeny

astł ařawōtin

inside of cells made of leftovers of the sword,
too familiar with hiding in nooks and crannies,
are the deoxyribonucleic markings
they hid - all other marking forbidden them -
spelling flame and Flood

all the efficiency that comes with ancience
shoveled into pyrin-printing at every
impulse to hide, or run

the woman's right to choose
which storm - protein or Sheykhalan
and no choice at all in what lies in wait for the sun
in the eastern province, where it arrives from
in the morning, where
men speak the stars in tongues, and poets
are born verdant and flowering

there a dragon lurks, between the sea
and the mountain, that he
might devour the sun
as soon as it is born

at the time of the end
there will be anguish
such as never was
since there first were nations

the vine, the fig tree, the pomegranate -
all the trees of the field
will dry up
and the stars will withdraw their shining

at the time of the end
he shall stand up, that secret father,
the great prince who stands watch
over your people
and he shall defeat the dragon which would
devour the sun being born;
the fruit of pomegranate, fig, grapevine

for by their fruit you will know them

lo, the third woe cometh quickly
rend your hearts and not your clothing

> *he that keeps my works to the end*
> *i will give the morning star*

three . sparśa

grammatology and plasticity

i would, yes, place two fingers
tenderly upon each trace
my fingers along your
search for words

i would also place two fingers
or perhaps the whole palm of a hand
against the untraced you
uncombed in the sweep
for what is left alive

not only alive

live charge collected
firing
thundering
to earth
to ground

your search for
ground

i would leave a trace
of fingers along you
words written
in the language your body speaks

every pulsating is embodied when you notice it

in abstraction the tongue made dull
the limbs to cramp
the fingers to rasp nervously, dumbly, at plastic meaningless icons
not even of words but of words fragmented into misleading dissections
a tenth grade textbook anatomy of the atom

only that which is precisely unusable available to me

or, as Martin might say, the *obtrusiveness* of every medium
at hand

every medium that is not my hand, or lips

i could push eight fingers into just beneath my collar-bone, let sink,
and with a hold, rend myself in tatters
to pull this quivering ache, this tremor-throb from behind my chest
for want of your trembling bones in mine

there is a cradling insisting upon itself throughout each fibrous strand of hand, arm, breast, shoulder,
the neck as it arcs the head toward what is held there at its heart-center

there is no use trying to convince a body of a thousand miles

you tell me you ache, and my heart sends every battalion to the holding-front
and leaves the speaking destitute

sparśa

with each thumb
alight upon   in the center of   the brow
mantra-pulse in threes
clearest elocution through the electrons at the outskirts of the fingers coming so near
the electrons at the outskirts of your skin that they repel one another with the force of
quantum avoidance, hovering so infinitesimally close our brains translate it as touch

or, in other words, touching the tips of our radiations together

mantra's true name is invoked only
if its word-name is kept secret
pulse in threes

with authority! the preacher declared, offering a farewell benediction
a well-earned claim after a lifetime of blessings
showed him the authority in every electron
with authority! pulse in threes

hold. gently
lift each thumb
bring lips to lips
then clearly, softly, speak a different mantra:
light upon   hover very, very close to   radiate toward

no unfitting husband

careful, crowded blue being
tenor and tonere, holding and resounding
like the dead
he cares for beings, not for doings

he holds in his lap my battered brain
holds in his mouth my shattered skin
lets Mercury guide his fingers
to spell *aniksi* across my belly,
the birth once known as the ear
which his Eustachian resonance is suited
precisely for

Al-Bāṭin become flesh in the manner
of *to know* become *glory* in the flesh
of tongue after tongue
he touches, holds, speaks
in tongues

he uncovers a secret womb in my tongue
and gently places his seeds upon it

a secret kind of heliotropism

watcher of the night, prince of nocturnal thunder,
Opertus, Quietalis, Aïdēs
most named of any of the unseen

the secret substance of the world of ghosts
offering sweet ruby abundance   yet unknown
even to the honey-maiden, goddess of fertile ground

        he wanted to show her the hidden mystery
        where he is at rest with himself and all creatures,
        spoke the man from whom God hid nothing

Amenthes, who has cycles of his own
who may live a year in an hour or live the same hour for 20,000 *years*

eternity is a long time to be alone
and in his aching head he forgets:
        he offers the maiden his jeweled seeds
        and becomes secret father to each spring

if you are the Son of God, you can only be so by having the same
being of God that the Son has. But this is now hidden from us, spoke the man
from whom God hid nothing

to my dearest mother Demeter, your daughter Kórē greets you.

it is with great rejoicing that i learn that i might be with you once again, for i long for your embrace, and for the beautiful ocean-edged fields of Nysa where i once found peace.

yet i must confess to you that alongside my joy i also hold a strange sorrow, for much to my surprise i have become fond of the cool, quiet realm to which i have been taken. and stranger yet, i have become fond of its prince as well. he lifts me to his side, promising me every right offered to the highest of the deathless gods, and asks me only to feel kindly toward him. i begin to feel i might trust him with the most secret parts of me.

i think, sweet mother, that i may be falling in love with this strange being of thunder, this chthonic host of many, this night watchman, this unseen prince, with whom i feel more seen than i ever did with what Helios lights by day.

he has offered me a taste of his fruit, jeweled richly with sweet, plentiful seeds, and i have partaken with great gladness. in two thirds of a year, i will bring forth the most abundant life. and do not be angered, nor shed a tear, for i will be with you for the greater part of that year, and all years henceforth. i will return only for a third of each to be with my husband, in the respite of our dark kingdom at the center of the earth, from which all life springs forth.

favor me by taking pity on me, and forgive me mother, for i have no choice but to become queen of this underworld - not because i was stolen away, but because i cannot do other than be guided by the love i know in my heart.

peace be with you until i can be with you myself.

The War of the Sons of Light Against the Sons of Darkness: the war of heaven

yet another name of the most named: *Dionysus*

the essence of indestructible life

the archangel, venerated as leader of the Army of God,
warrior of the spiritual battle within

the archangel fights a dragon, hurls it to earth
for daring to attempt to harm the woman clothed with the sun
and with the moon under her feet; for daring
to attempt to consume the child being born of her

you shall have the greatest rights among the deathless gods
for you, Persephone, I will be no unfitting husband

and he was received by a virgin who was a wife
and was born verdant and flowering with his entire divinity,
spoke the man from whom God hid nothing

the angel of death, who is the word, comes to each soul at the hour of dying
and offers it a chance for redemption before it turns
that corner

he escorts every soul to its passing, and in his scales which are held by the maiden
he weighs them each, the great mysterious Seer of all men

he is judge and shepherd, word and messenger,
guardian and warrior, lover and healer,
the source of life and of a secret kind of life

Mikha'El   not yet born, but being born

                spoke the man from whom God hid nothing: we are
                an only son   whom the Father has been eternally begetting
                out of the hidden darkness of eternal concealment

Just as flowers turn their heads towards the sun, so too does that which has been turned, by virtue of a
secret kind of heliotropism, towards the sun which is dawning in the sky of history.

-Walter Benjamin, *On the Concept of History*

four . somaheliosophy

somaheliosophy

sunlight hazy sifting into earthen material
presence   waves emanating
from a being so still and old
so alive and radiant
a fission-being   as much
its radiation as its core
always a wave and always a particle   in every fractal

springtime ripples pull light out of hidden

deep places under rocks and pebbles

deeper than a creek is expected

to be   in the quiet surging rush of snow-melt

ancient mithraic sight
grounded, but ethereal
by its subcutaneous familiarity
by its contact with the eternal

the sun is not dead   it has only scattered
a diaspora i recognize in the nape of my neck
in the heart chakra
in the lines pigment traces in my skin

with reference to Michael S. Judge's 'necroheliosophy'

flailing isn't failing!

cogito ergo sum - a man untethered
from reality
finds a foothold in the very fact of flailing for one

betrayal of fidelity to the Event: he builds false idols
but false only in the failure to realize
the way in which what he found was god   he made an idol
                                                of   not the thing which flails
                                                and of   not the flailing

a false idol, an image of the Idea
of the thing which flails
of the thing which ideates
of the thing which *cogita*

an image not only of, but not of

the foundational error   but when the image exits, God enters
                                          spoke the man from whom god hid nothing

Marathon Taverna

impact asteroidal enough to return me
to the drawing-board,
lacquered wood and pool tables i have to reach
halfway to the fifth grade to remember

ten years has at least taught me the difference
between holding and holding-onto;
what she meant by poetry;
what i mean by poetry -

> i wrote such clinging into, out of,
> this blessed stuffy hole
> but he deserved the kind of words
> i write for you, the miracle-resounding
> of the music of the spheres that's in your cavities
> when i let the angel conduct my pencil -

ten years, that is, or you

at the bottom of it all, a sorrow -

                    barren, or simply bare? -

twisting its way beneath every year,
every poem

a sorrow only men recognize, or almost-only
at least

                              i'm never gonna know you now

and a holding even fewer understand

                              but i'm gonna love you anyhow

blue Tuesdays, blue Fridays, blue lightning
always, always some kind of April
testing for the precise amount of Aries in the moon
(having long ago learned not to look directly at the sun)
that will charge without burning

no sleep 'til

crinkled   eyes, brows
early-aged heart revealed in the manner of
blue youth-skin
and careful glee

Brooklyn

the place where i have what it takes

xo, mom
inscribed on his arm, or his soul

the facets of the light left in this world

           - keeping in mind always that the sun
            is not dead   it has only scattered -

are all blue

for M
for T
for Elliott
for Anne

that sudden structural harmony

"To remain with the dead is to abandon them.
All the years I felt Bella entreating me, filled with her loneliness, I was mistaken. I have misunderstood her signals. Like other ghosts, she whispers; not for me to join her, but so that, when I'm close enough, she can push me back into the world.*"*

-Anne Michaels, Fugitive Pieces

                            those centuries of you holding me

eternity is a long time to be alone

                            i tried and tried
                            something holding me to the Earth

not only alive
your search for ground

                            it's hard to disbelieve
                            I don't know how, baby
                            god, I'm sorry, I just don't know how

in his aching head he forgets
the sun   is not dead
waves emanating   *the facets of the light left in this world*
live charge collected
thundering
to ground

lay in my lap your
aching head
battered too young to learn
how to myelinate
leaking blue being
but only red for blood

he cries   *god grant me only a drop*
                                      to cool my tongue
and he touches, holds, speaks
in tongues

                                  my skin is weeping salt and acid
                                  for want of someone to touch me kindly
dyshidrotic weeping to teach the eyes
he that hath skin, let him hear
            eisegesis error → neurotic dermatillomania

lay in my lap your shattered skin
i would trace along your search
for sparśa   uncover
the bones-star shining   *UP FROM UNDERGROUND*

grounded, but ethereal
by its subcutaneous familiarity

the sun is not dead
it has only shattered

                              he gives what he most needs

darkness has fallen, and births shine forth
slowly goes the boat of Ra

seven candles, one altar, two priests -
both women, but neither of them priestesses -

one cup from which to drink the light
which heals -   shining *UP FROM UNDERGROUND*
in its passage to the return

of the sun

                    (remembering always that the sun
                    is not dead   it has only
                    bled   to bring life into this world
                    and has entered her rivers to be reborn)

one hand pointing skyward; one outward, open

christ
in you

                    (and he was received by a virgin who was a wife
                    and was born verdant and flowering with his entire divinity,
                    spoke the man from whom god hid nothing)

one cup   alive   teeming
touched by lip after lip
the true sacred revealed

        etym. *reveal*:
                from Latin *revēlāre*, "to reveal, uncover,"
                from *re-*, "back, again" + *vēlāre*, "to cover,"
                        from *vēlum*, "veil"

the true sacred unveiled
in the unmasking of those lips

the peace
be   in you

unveiled, we encounter -   a priest and a priestess
                             a woman and a woman
                             an elder and a younger
                             a vessel and a vessel

christ
in you

                    (remembering always that the son
                    is not dead   it is only being born)

rejoice, Virgo, full of grace
blessed is the fruit of thy womb

शान्तिः शान्तिः शान्तिः